By your Traditions

But Not by God's Word

A Theological Perspective Against Arguments and Actions Opposing and Hindering Women in the Gospel Ministry

Reverend Arthur D. Griffin, *Th.D., D.D.*

BLACK LIGHT FELLOWSHIP

Chicago, Illinois

By Your Traditions, but Not by God's Word
A Theological Perspective Against Arguments and Actions
Opposing and Hindering Women in the Gospel Ministry

Second Edition 1993
First Printing 1993

Cover Design: Troy Brown Design

Publisher:

BLACK LIGHT FELLOWSHIP
128 S. Paulina Street · Chicago, IL 60612
P.O. Box 5369 · Chicago, IL 60680
312.563.0081

ISBN: 0-933176-39-2

LC: 93-7353

Library of Congress Cataloging-in-Publication Data

Griffin, Arthur D.
By your traditions, but not by God's word : a theological perspective against arguments and actions opposing and hindering women in the gospel ministry / Arthur D. Griffin, -- 2nd ed.
p. cm.
Rev. ed. of: By your traditions.
ISBN 0-933176-39-2 :
1. Ordination of women. I. Griffin, Arthur D. By your traditions.
II. Title.
BV676.G75 1993
262',14'082--dc20 93-7353

Manufactured in the United States of America.

98 97 96 95 94 93
10 9 8 7 6 5 4 3 2 1

By your Traditions

But Not by God's Word

A Theological Perspective Against Arguments and Actions Opposing and Hindering Women in the Gospel Ministry

"Thus have ye made

the commandment of God of none

effect by your tradition."

The Gospel of St. Matthew 15:6b

Table of Contents

Black Light Fellowship

Chicago, Illinois

I agree with Rev McClary the Bible supports the full freedom

But there is no Biblical proof texts to show that Christ calls women into the Gospel pastoral leadership Ministry!

Foreword

The words and works of most prophets and of those who maintain a prophetical outlook in their generation are seldom fully appreciated until these gifted and godly spokespersons have passed from the scene. Nevertheless, without a vision the people perish. It has not been without a prophetic genius that Reverend Doctor Arthur D. Griffin has taken pen to hand in order to wrestle with one of the burning issues facing especially traditional Black Baptist Churches and numerous others: the role of women in the Gospel ministry. It is worth noting that his words follow on the heels of having taken a firm stance over the years supporting the full freedom of women in the Church to exercise all the gifts of the Holy Spirit as God alone sees fit. His words match his works.

As a highly academically qualified theologian with exceptional credentials, not to overlook the passionate spiritual fervor and insight he possesses, Reverend Doctor Griffin has employed both his skills and his graces as he addresses this theological, controversial, and revolutionary subject. He speaks with much clarity, profundity and conviction to his own colleagues in the pastoral ministry. The author challenges all Christian ministers to cooperate with our sovereign God with respect to His bestowal of gifts, call, ordination and the support of women in preaching the Gospel of Christ Jesus, despite our traditions. **By Your Traditions** is a message whose time has come. It is long overdue.

The purpose of **Black Light Fellowship** is to publish and disseminate Christian Black biblical literature, and to share the message in this literature with as many people as possible. It is with great pleasure that we present and commend **By Your Traditions** to our readers. Its tone bespeaks that liberating theological and Scriptural dimension needed by Black Churches and believers for their spiritual renewal, social freedom, and cultural progress.

Reverend Walter Arthur McCray, *Director*
Black Light Fellowship, *Chicago, Illinois*

By your Traditions

But Not by God's Word

Reverend Arthur D. Griffin, *Th.D., D.D.*

Prophecy (1 Cor

is for the edifying

the Church 1 Cor 14:3-4, 5
the Church those who 12, 17, understanding in
Those - by Prophesying believe (anyone)
In Christ, those who will benefit
and say "Amen"

- Evangelist, Pastors and teachers are for determining and delineating the truth of God's word from false teachers:

- by Revelation
- by knowledge
- by teaching
- by prophesying

} Eph

So is prophesying = delivering God's Message to God's people? or determining truth of The Bible in face of Satan's

Chapter 1

God's Call is God's Prerogative

The objective of this publication is to expose the subtle and sophisticated deception perpetrated on the Church by Satan through the **traditions of men** that **denies** the Holy Spirit the right to dispense the spiritual gifts of prophecy and exhortation to whomever He wills. We submit that He **alone** makes such determinations, and we humans must cease and desist from quenching and limiting Him by our ignorance of His will and way; simply because we don't understand it or appreciate it! In fact, we all need to learn to shut our mouths; to mind our own business, and to wholly submit ourselves to the **absolute** control of the Holy Spirit; for only **then** can we honestly say to Him: Have Thine own way, Lord; in **my** life, and in **Your** Church!

When we come to this level of spiritual maturity, the exercise of the gifts of prophecy and exhortation by women and anyone else the Holy Spirit bestows them upon will no longer be opposed by us but welcomed with open arms! Indeed, these gifted persons will be happily and gratefully welcomed because the harvest is **still great** and the laborers are **still few**! However, many of us are still praying the Lord of the harvest "that he will send forth labourers into his harvest" (Matthew 9:38b), and we **are not so presumptuous** as to **refuse** those He sends because of their race, sex, color, education, or cultural differences. Anyone who **does** is in **desperate** need of a change of mind; for obviously, he does not understand the value of the harvest of human souls to God; what it costs Him to make that harvest possible, and why the Holy Spirit must be in **complete** control of the vineyard **and** the laborers. They are both so precious to the Lord!

The Lord has bestowed upon His Church many a spiritually-gifted person, and to each believer He has endowed with at least one spiritual gift (cf. 1 Corinthians 12:4-6; Romans 12:6-8; Ephesians 4:7-13; 1 Corinthians 12:28-31; 1 Corinthians 12:7-11). Without question, it is the clear Scriptural teaching that God has bestowed these gifts upon His Church irrespective of a believer's gender or social status in life. Women who are Christians are endowed with the gifts of the Spirit just as men. The gifts of "prophecy," "exhortation," and even the spiritual ability to just simply "testify" are the gifts we choose to highlight (cf. Acts 2:17-18, 40).

For years, we have refused to address the **problem**; for it has been more comfortable and convenient for us to ignore it; to sweep it under the rug; to pass it off as a "controversy" wherein there were differences of opinion within our ranks, and literally to "write off" from our fellowship those in our denominational family who did not see it the way we did. However, this approach to the problem has not provided for us a solution; nor indeed can it; for, we do not always share unanimity even in our understanding of Scripture, and so we continue to have differences of opinion and difficulty with those who do not see it the way we do. That is why a **definitive statement from God** that does not necessitate **human** interpretation—because it is clear cut—is so vital to a successful resolution to the problem.

The Scriptures provide us with such a definitive statement in Joel 2:28-29:

> And it shall come to pass afterward, that I will pour out of my spirit upon all flesh, and your sons **and your daughters** shall prophesy, your old men shall dream dreams, your young men shall see visions and also upon the servants **and** upon the **handmaids** in those days will I pour out of my spirit.

This direct word from the mouth of the Lord is reiterated in Acts 2:15-18:

> But this is that which was spoken by the prophet Joel: And it shall come to pass in the last days **saith God**, I will pour out of my spirit upon all flesh, and your sons **and your daughters** shall prophesy, and your young men shall see visions, and your old men shall dream dreams, and on my servants **and on my handmaidens**, I will pour out in those days of my spirit, and they shall prophesy.

There is no need to interpret, and no need to elaborate; for this says what it means and means what it says! When

God says, "I do!" and we say, "I don't!" there should be no question in our minds as to who is right and who is wrong. **God** is right, and **we** are wrong! If, after reading this book, the reader still has not read or heard anything that has caused him to change his mind, let him and anyone else whose mind remains intransigent consider this direct word from the mouth of the Lord!

Persistence on our part to deny the Holy Spirit **full** control over the distribution and exercise of the gift of prophesy so clearly delineated by these two Scriptures escalates our discussion of this matter from the realm of "**controversy**" to the realm of the problem. If, having considered Joel 2:28-29 and Acts 2:15-18, **anyone** still holding to the **traditions of men** that deny the gift of prophecy to women, let it be clearly understood that **they themselves** are the "**problem**"; for they have closed their minds to the truth of **God's direct word**, and it is a very tragic thing to have a closed mind!

There are many truths that are clearly elucidated in the Scriptures that many of us see with no trouble whatsoever; while others, to the very **same** truths will say, "I just don't see that at all," and women in the Gospel Ministry is one of such truths! It really should not be necessary to defend the calling of women in the Gospel Ministry any more than it should be necessary to defend the calling of **men**; for both are "one in Christ" to be used as the Holy Spirit sees fit to use them, and that is not the real intent of this book. It is rather my intention to remind those who hold that God cannot or will not send a woman into this area of Christian service, that either wittingly or unwittingly they trample underfoot the authority, sovereignty, and omnipotence of God by presuming to tell Him what He can and cannot do! Would it be a sin for God to use a woman in His service as a preacher of His Word? Is God limited as to whom He can use? Who set such limitations upon Him? Isn't it true that those persons whom God calls He also spiritually equips to do His work?

The questions posed above raise a larger and more fundamental question that transcends them in significance and importance to our faith; for they represent a very sophisticated, subtle but obvious satanic attack on the authority, sovereignty, and omnipotence of God, **and this is the real issue** that must be addressed! This subtle attack seeks to get the Church to focus Her attention and interest on the **messenger** when Her concern and interest ought to be directed to the **message**! This represents a very shrewd diversionary tactic of the devil; for, the Church is busy expending its energy and time debating the **calling** of ministers, which is **exclusively** the business of the Holy Spirit, instead of taking care of the business Christ left in our hands to implement, and that is:

> Go ye therefore, and teach all nations, baptizing them in the name of the Father, and of the Son, and of the Holy Ghost: teaching them to observe all things whatsoever I have commanded you: and, lo, I am with you alway, even unto the end of the world. Amen (Matthew 28:19-20).

Consistency and Christian integrity demand that if through our churches we take pleasure in ordaining called and gifted men into the Gospel ministry, that we should also take the same pleasure in so ordaining called and gifted women.

We recognize that there **are** persons whose minds can **never** be changed about **anything** they strongly believe in; they sometimes call it "conviction," but God calls it "stiff-necked"! They sometimes call it "principle" but God calls it "stubbornness"! But are such "convictions" and "principles" biblically founded, or are these good terms merely employed to masquerade deep prejudices? It is difficult for us human beings to **admit** we are wrong, and so to "save face" we pretend there is nothing new for us to learn from God and His Word. There are countless thousands of members in the Body of Christ who are going to find it necessary to swallow their pride and simply admit that they have been wrong concerning the prophetic role of women in the Kingdom of God. Traditions born from the opinions of men have always caused dissension and division within the Body of Christ; the very fact that these two related passages of Scripture **unite** men and women in the equality of spiritual blessings attests that they did not originate with **men**, but with **God**!

To begin with, **all** men must realize that truth is truth, whether they **see** it or not or whether they **understand** it or not—it is still the **truth**! Of course, it is characteristic of human beings to measure the perception of truth by others with their own ability to perceive it. In other words, we think it **highly** improbable that others can see greater revelations in the Word of God than we have seen, and so we seek to limit their level of perception and understanding of Scripture to that of our own. We must all come to the realization that the higher up you go upon the mountain, the more you will see; and even after your vision has projected you to the point where the sky joins the horizon, there is always still a lot more to see even beyond that point.

Men at the foot of the mountain or even halfway up cannot possibly have the same overview as those who are approaching or standing on its summit; and correspondingly, men of limited theological exposure, training, and perception cannot see what is crystal clear to those who have had such exposure, training, and spiritual discipline; for their perceptions have been enhanced and enlarged even beyond their highest expectations through such exposure, training, and discipline. However, when you don't know—you just don't know. But it is difficult to deal with a person who doesn't know and doesn't **know** that he does not know! The spiritual ignorance that makes our "not knowing" so **catastrophic** in this instance is because we are guilty of quenching the Spirit from effectively using those He desires to use for the spreading of the Gospel, and that is a very **serious** indignity against His Personage!

Furthermore, we must come to grips with God's assertion to **all** men—including those who became Apostles—and all succeeding generations of saints in the Church: "My ways are not your ways; neither my thoughts your thoughts; as the heavens are higher than the earth; so are my thoughts over your thoughts, and my ways over your ways" (Isaiah 55:8). Again, the Lord says to us: "And it shall come to pass afterward, that I will pour out of my spirit upon all flesh; and your sons **and your daughters** shall prophesy; your old men shall dream dreams, your young men shall see visions; and also upon the servants and upon **the handmaids** in those days will I pour out of my spirit" (Joel 2:28-29). The Apostle Peter reiterated this prophecy on the Day of Pentecost, calling the filling of the Church with the Holy Ghost as "that which was spoken by the Prophet Joel: and it shall come to pass in the last days, **saith God**, I will pour out of my spirit upon all flesh: and your sons **and your daughters** shall prophesy, and your young men shall see visions, and your old men shall dream dreams: and on my servants and **on my handmaidens** I will pour out in those days of my spirit: **and they shall prophesy**" (Acts 2:16-18).

Those who dogmatically oppose the role of the "daughters" in the ministry of prophecy because they are not quite **sure** of what is right—despite the clear and unmistakable pronouncement by Peter that "**daughters**" as well as sons would share such a role "in the last days, saith God"—such persons would do well to consider the wisdom of Gamaliel, the great doctor of Law, distinguished member of the Sanhedrin, and mentor of Saul of Tarsus. In Acts 5:33-39, when the Sanhedrin was deliberating as to which side was right as it related to the Apostles preaching the Messiahship of Jesus of Nazareth, Gamaliel, in wisdom, cautioned the Sanhedrin with the following words: "And now I say unto you, refrain from these men, and let them alone: for if this counsel or the work be of men; it will come to nought. But if it be of God, ye cannot overthrow it; lest haply ye be found even to fight against God" (Acts 5:38-39). Gamaliel's advice to the Sanhedrin has tremendous relevance to the Church today as it relates to whether the Spirit of God gives to women the gifts of prophecy and exhortation, and the

Church would do well to heed it; lest haply **we** "be found even to fight against God." Let us today refrain from these women, and let them alone; for if **their** counsel or if **their** work be of themselves, it will soon come to nought. But if it be of God, ye cannot overthrow it!

Moreover, we must remember that our God is a God of mercy; so His sharing the richness of His spiritual gifts with human beings is one of the most profound acts of mercy presented in His Word, and it is He Himself who says, "I will have mercy on whom I will have mercy, and I will have compassion on whom I will have compassion" (Romans 9:15). Indeed, for **most** Christians, **that settles that**!

The number one reason for opposing the ordained prophetic role of women can be expressed in one sentence: "**Traditionally**, the Church has held that the place of women was not in the pulpit." Perhaps it would be **more** accurate to say that **many people** in the Church have **traditionally** held that the place of women was not in the pulpit. Also, it might be more accurate to say that **some** denominations in the Church have held that the **traditional** place of women was not in the pulpit; to which Jesus, Head of the Church, would respond: "**By your tradition**, you make null and void the word of God" (cf. Matthew 15:6; Mark 7:13).

It is an established fact that we live in a male-dominated society even today, and any student of ancient history will attest that male domination was a thousand times more severe in biblical times than today. To cite a few cases in point: In ancient times, women were considered the **property** of men, so a man could have as many wives as he could afford; but a woman could have only one husband. The genealogies listed in the Bible give the generations of **men**—never the women, and even in New Testament times, it was the **woman** taken "in the very act of adultery" and brought before Jesus to be stoned; no such judgment was put upon the man. Yet all of us understand that there had to be a man involved in the transgression, but there is no mention of him in the entire narrative.

No, men cannot blame God for their prejudices, or for the prejudices they found in society before they arrived on the scene; whether those prejudices are racial, cultural, sexual, or geographical, they are the results of man's **sin** and **not** the will of God! Indeed, it is true that we suffer from these prejudices because of ignorance and failure to correctly ascertain the mind of God on this subject and any **other** subject that causes us to deny **anyone** their inalienable rights!

There are those who hasten to remind us of the many scholarly and saintly men who have been guilty of this kind of prejudice, and simply because they were scholarly and saintly we should not question the wrongness of their prejudice. They chide us for asserting that they have been wrong all those years as the height of affrontery. But despite the chiding, they were **still wrong**; and it isn't the first time the **whole** counsels of God have proven them wrong, nor will it be the last time! Indeed, it does not come as any surprise to serious students of God's Word to learn that when it comes to the things of the Spirit and truths of spiritual dimensions, man is wrong **most of the time**! Our sinful perversion always puts us in antithesis to God's will and God's way; so you can depend on man to be going west when God is going east in terms of almost

everything; and certainly, God's right to use whom He will—including **women and children**—for the work of the ministry and the preaching of the Gospel is an excellent case in point. How **often** must we be reminded that our ways are not His ways, nor our thoughts His thoughts!

Again, many people would take us through the Genesis account of the fall of man and the subsequent judgment of God upon man, the woman, and the serpent as proof that the place of women is one of subjection, and so the obvious conclusion is that they therefore cannot be the recipients of the spiritual gifts of prophecy and exhortation from the Holy Spirit. Others take upon themselves the authority to proclaim that no one can deal honestly with Scripture and conclude otherwise to what they conclude! Thank the Lord, the Holy Spirit is God, and therefore knows all things; because if He didn't, this conclusion would come as a real shock to Him, since He has been using women as Ambassadors of the Kingdom all these years.

To be sure, there are many traditional reasons for holding that the place of women was not in the pulpit, but there are no **biblical or theological reasons** for upholding this tradition; and if you question those who support this tradition you will soon discover that **all** of their arguments are **physical/social** and completely ignore the more important **spiritual** realities. That fact alone is enough to show the falacious nature of their tradition, and why it is by their tradition that they make null and void the Word of God.

The gifts of prophecy and exhortation—**preaching**, if you will—are **spiritual gifts**, given and administered exclusively by the Holy Spirit to do **spiritual** battle against a **spiritual** enemy and to edify and nourish the Lord's **spiritual Body**—the Church! You cannot fight a spiritual enemy with physical weapons, and you cannot edify and nourish a spiritual Body with physical food; so the emphasis must never be upon the **messenger**, but upon the **message!** As long as the devil can keep our eyes on the physical/social levels, he keeps us from seeing where the action **really is**, and away from where the strategies and policies are formed. That puts us at a distinct disadvantage in our struggles against principalities, powers, rulers of the darkness of this world, and spiritual wickedness in high places.

Unfortunately, those who see the Holy Spirit's use of women in His ministering service as **contrary** to God's will are addressing and discussing the issue, as Nicodemus tried to do with Jesus in another spiritual issue, from a dimension of **the flesh** or **physical** realities, while they should be addressing it from a dimension of the **spiritual realities**, as all important matters concerning the Church **must** be addressed. Therefore, we too must remind them, as Jesus did Nicodemus: "That which is flesh is flesh, and that which is spirit is spirit." Let us discuss spiritual realities on a **spiritual** level; for that is what we must be about if we are to see and understand God's will and God's way. There is a distinct dichotomy between the physical and the spiritual, and one must come to understand that the spiritual dimensions both created and control the physical dimensions; so the spiritual is greater. That is why Paul says, "We look not at the things which are seen; but the things which are not seen: for the things which are seen are temporal: but the things which are not seen as eternal" (2 Corinthians 4:18). "Through faith we understand that the worlds were framed by the word of God, so that things which are seen were not made of things which do appear" (Hebrews 11:3).

Chapter 2

Saving Souls or Segregating Women?

The spiritual dimension of life and ministry is important and preeminent. Such a spiritual dimension was emphasized by Jesus during His earthly ministry, and it caused violent opposition from the religious leaders of Israel. When they complained about His disciples eating with unwashed hands (a physical concern), Jesus countered: "Hear and understand: not that which goeth **into** the mouth defileth a man: but that which cometh **out** of the mouth defileth a man" (Matthew 15:11). The writer of Proverbs said, "Keep thy **heart** with all diligence: for out of **it** are the issues of life" (Proverbs 4:23). Again, Jesus incurred the wrath of the religious leaders because He gave proper emphasis and importance of the spiritual over the physical in evaluating **their** positions as leaders. He said,

> Ye blind guides, which strain at a gnat, and swallow a camel. Woe unto you, scribes and pharisees, hypocrites! For ye make clean the outside of the cup

and of the platter; but within they are full of extortion and excess. Thou blind pharisee, cleanse first that which is within the cup and platter, that the outside of them may be clean also. Woe unto you, scribes and pharisees, hypocrites! For ye are like unto whited sepulchres which indeed appear beautiful outward: but are within full of dead men's bones, and of all uncleanness. Even so ye also outwardly appear righteous unto men, but within ye are full of hypocrisy and iniquity (Matthew 23:24-28).

Today, we strain at a gnat (women in the Gospel Ministry) and swallow a camel (souls that would have been reached by the preaching of the Gospel by women, but now lost in hell or on their way to eternal perdition). It doesn't bother us that, by the ungodly, senseless stupidity of our sexual prejudice and traditions, we quench the Holy Spirit by cutting from His disposal this valuable resource that He would use. We show ourselves to be little men who are concerned over the outside of the cup and platter—the physical, the gender of the person —instead of being mindful of the more important inside or spirit as an instrument that the Holy Spirit can use to present the Gospel of salvation to the lost!

Precious souls, lost forever in eternity because the **one** messenger of God they would have positively responded to just happened to be born a **woman** instead of a man. But by our tradition, we forbid women access to preach from the pulpit of the Church; so the message never goes forth at that special time for that special person!

In a well-known publication, a minister sarcastically remarked he found it strange that in recent times so many women were getting the "call" to the ministry; to which the Church would respond: "Praise the Lord!" For years we have been praying for more laborers in the vineyard as the Lord commanded us, and now He is answering our prayer; for we had sense enough not to try to dictate to Him whether they should be young or old, black or white, male or female, rich or poor, educated or uneducated, short or tall; or any other **physical** restraints. No, we simply prayed for Him to send laborers into His harvest of human souls, and we praise Him for honoring our sincere prayers! It would appear that common sense would dictate, even to the untrained rational mind, that if a soul is as important to God as the Scripture definitively proclaims, and if it is a fact that Jesus said, "For what is a man profited, if he shall gain the whole world, and lose his own soul? Or what shall a man give in exchange for his soul?" Does it not stand to reason that the Holy Spirit would not overlook this vast resource of consecrated Christian women to bestow upon them the gifts of prophecy and exhortation. They outnumber men in most of our churches by a three-, four-, or five-to-one ratio, and since, as we read in 1 Corinthians 1:21b, "It pleased God by the foolishness of preaching to save them that believe."

Does it violate the character of God to use women to preach His Gospel for the salvation of them that believe? Of course not! Whenever little men attribute **"nots"** to the Eternal, Sovereign, and Almighty God of Heaven and Earth, you **immediately** know they have had no theological training or the most basic theological disciplines to help them understand what little children and the most uneducated and untutored member in the

Church can understand and appropriate by faith with no problem at all. So when these little men of limited understanding say that the Holy Spirit does **not**, can**not**, will **not**, must **not**, should **not**, would **not** or put upon Him any **other** restrictions, restraints, or prohibitions, they seek to transfer to **Him** the limitations of their **own humanity**, and that is **so** pitiful!

The "nots" that can be applied to the Holy Spirit are those that violate His character; for instance, the Holy Spirit can**not** sin, because He is perfect holiness. The Holy Spirit can**not** die, because He is eternal in His existence. These and many other characteristics and attributes belong to His **Personage** and therefore are **immutable**! However, the Holy Spirit's use of women or even children as His ambassadors does not have **anything** to do with His attributes, character, or personage; for these are everlasting and existed in complete perfection before He created **anything** in Heaven or Earth. It is the epitome of stupidity for any man to dictate to the Holy Spirit what He **can** or **cannot** do; who He **can** or **cannot** call; whom He **will**, or **will not** use! In fact, if it was not born of **sheer ignorance**, it would be blasphemous! We are well within our prerogatives and rights to ask such persons: Just **who** do you think you **are**? When did God give **you** the **authority** to call His Ambassadors?

Ambassadors don't appoint or select ambassadors even in human systems of government; so when the Scriptures ask, "How shall they preach, except they be sent?" (Romans 10:15a), the **Sender** is not the Church; nor other preachers; nor is it the denomination. The Sender is the Holy Spirit; He **alone** determines who shall be sent forth to preach the Gospel, and the gifts He distributes for the enabling of this ministry are called **prophecy and exhortation**! (Romans 12:3-8; Ephesians 4:11; 1 Corinthians 12:8-10, 28-30)

Many persons who oppose women being the recipients of the gifts of prophecy and exhortation feel they must genuinely do so to **"protect"** the Church from unscrupulous women who would use the authority of the gifts to the detriment of the Body of Christ. A similar concern was reflected in the history of the early Church, particularly with the first century called-out-ones, when pagan religious practices still exerted a very strong influence as part of the dominant culture surrounding them. The role of women as priests, vestial virgins, and temple prostitutes was a definite problem for the Apostolic Church Period, for it would have been **so** easy for such women to infiltrate and destroy the very moral fabric of the infant Church fellowships.

Therefore, one can readily understand and even appreciate the reaction of the Church against women participating in **any** leadership position or service within the Fellowship, and so much caution was well-advised.

However, thanks be to God, we have learned that our defense is the Holy Spirit Himself, and if we obey Him and follow His leadership, **He** will not only defend the Body of Christ but give it enabling power to **overcome** the spiritual attacks of the evil one that show up in human weaknesses and emphasis on physical concerns and interests. This concern, born out of Jewish temple worship tradition and coupled with concern for fear of contemporary pagan influence, moved an aberrant group of very weak and carnal churches at Corinth to hold the position: "Let your women keep silence in the churches:

for it is not permitted unto them to speak: but they are commanded to be under obedience, **as also saith the law**. And if they will learn anything, let them ask their husbands at home: for it is a shame for women to speak in the church" (1 Corinthians 14:34-35).

Yes! It was indeed a misguided Corinthian Church who spoke this slogan quoted by the Apostle Paul. This statement did not originate with Paul and neither did it express his position about the role of women in the Church. In fact, Paul's answer to these aberrant Corinthians is found in the very next verses where he expresses his apostolic outrage at such a narrow-minded distortion-of-the-Word-of-God view: "What? came the word of God out from you? or came it unto you only? If any man think himself to be a prophet, or spiritual, let him acknowledge that the things that I write unto you are the commandments of the Lord" (1 Corinthians 14:36-37). It was the male Corinthians, not Paul, who were transgressing the commandments of the Lord by disallowing women the privilege of exercising their God-ordained and rightful role in the fellowship and ministry of the Christian Church. Just like Jesus, Paul was promotive of the freedom of women in the Church. [Space does not permit a detailed exegesis of the varied Corinthian beliefs recited and refuted by the Apostle Paul in this epistle. They can be studied in the following passages: 1 Corinthians 1:12; 3:4; 6:12; 10:23; 6:13, 18; 7:1; 8:1; 8:8. Students of Greek should study carefully the grammar used by Paul, including the *e* conjunction as used in the following passages: 1 Corinthians 6:1-2; 6:9; 6:16 (twice); 9:6; 9:8; 9:10; 10:22; 11:13; and 14:33b-36.]

It is interesting that those who use this Scripture as proof against the prophetic participation of women apply the prohibition to them only in the **pulpit**, when the Scripture clearly states that "it is not permitted unto them to **speak**." They are not to **talk at all in the Church**, not even to ask a question in public, but "let them ask their husbands at home" if there is something they want to learn! To apply this rule to our churches today would mean no women singers in the choirs; no women presidents over groups and auxiliaries; no teachers, directors, superintendents, missionaries, or any other position of service wherein they break the **rule of silence**! At least those who oppose women in the pulpit could be **consistent** and obey the mandate **completely** and not just **in part**! Indeed, when Paul recited this Corinthian slogan, there were no formal "pulpits" as we now position them in the church edifices today; so women were to keep quiet in the church **whenever** they were sitting or standing. Even the most recalcitrant traditionalist cannot go along with so strict a literal application of these verses to the present-day church, and **neither** would the Apostle Paul.

Indeed, the very same Paul who refuted the wayward Corinthians, once he came to understand that the administration of the Church and the multiplicities of its ministries are exclusively in the hands of Holy Spirit, and that the Spirit is not hampered by the racial, sexual, geographical, or cultural prejudices of men, but in His mercy extends His blessings of spiritual gifts to **all** humanity, as **He** sees fit, then Paul could say, "There is neither Jew nor Greek, there is neither bond nor free, there neither male nor female: for ye all are **one** in Christ

Jesus!" (Galatians 3:28) One should note that it was the Lord Himself Who corrected the erroneous Judaistic views of the Apostle Paul. This occurred at the time of Paul's conversion to Christ, and especially during the three-year period Paul spent in the Arabian desert relearning his theology at the feet of Jesus (cf. Galatians 1:15-17ff.; 2:1ff.; 2 Corinthians 12:1-5). Since the epistle to the Galatians was the earliest New Testament writing, dated around 45 A.D., the Christian theology of Paul was well formulated when he declared the equality of all followers of Christ.

In the light of this declaration by the Apostle Paul, the question always arises: Why does Paul appear to counsel Timothy against women messengers? We have to emulate the patience and long-suffering of God with all men, **including** the Apostle Paul in the pragmatic implementation of what we **know** is God's will and God's way. It is one thing to **know** it; it is quite another thing to **do** it! In Paul's case, Galatians 3:28 makes a classic example for us to see this problem. Paul exclaims: "There is neither Jew nor Greek," but although Paul **could** grasp that truth **intellectually**, he had real difficulty in his early ministry putting it into **practice** in his cultural setting. The Church at-large shared this difficulty. It must be said to Paul's credit that he was able to do it **long** before the **other** apostles, in spite of the fact that God had made this truth plain in the Scriptures, and to cite a few examples: Genesis 12:3; 22:18; 49:10; Psalms 22:27; 68:31; 86:9; Isaiah 2:2-4; 9:2; 40:5; 42:1; 49:6; 60:3; Daniel 7:14; Malachi 1:11; Matthew 8:11-21; Luke 21:24; John 10:16; Acts 9:15.

Indeed, Paul **knew** God's will and way in this matter, but it was not until he and Barnabas were confronted by the callous recalcitrance and unbelief of their Jewish brethren was he literally **forced** to say: "It was necessary that the word of God should first have been spoken to you: but seeing ye put it from you, and judge yourselves unworthy of everlasting life, lo, **we turn to the Gentiles**. For so hath the Lord commanded us, saying, I have set thee to be a light of the Gentiles, that thou shouldest be for salvation unto the ends of the earth and when the Gentiles heard this they were glad, and glorified the word of the Lord: and as many as were ordained to eternal life believed" (Acts 13:46-48).

The point we want to get across is that even though Paul could understand the theological concept that the Gospel was for **Gentiles** as well as **Jews**, perhaps initially and **practically** he had real problems sharing the Gospel of Jesus with **non-Jews or Gentiles**. His **practices** did not match his **theology** until he was constrained by God through stubborn Jewish unbelief to turn to the Gentiles!

Further, Paul explains "there is neither bond nor free"; but here again Paul the **theologian** is way ahead of Paul the **churchman**, and the churchman has a real problem in the implementation of the pragmatic in spite of God's revelation to him that in Christ "there is neither bond nor free." Consider the case of Paul sending Onesimus back to Philemon for him to accept again Onesimus as a brother. Due to Roman law Paul had to still recognize Philemon's **ownership** of Onesimus as a **slave** and, therefore, Paul sent him back to his **owner**. But according to Christian theology, Onesimus was to be treated as a brother "in humanity"; and moreover as a brother "in the Lord" (Philemon 16). Ipso facto, according to Christian theology, Onesimus was free.

We are not hard on Paul, for slavery was an institutionalized part of society even within the **Christian community**, and in this case Paul the theologian and Paul the churchman are fairly consistent with each other. For though Paul honestly felt, in order to maintain the integrity of the Christian faith from those who would "pimp-off" the Church's freedom in Christ, that a person should keep on with the work he was doing when the Lord called him, Paul concludes, by stating whatever situation (servant or bond-servant) a person is in when he **becomes** a Christian, let him stay there. Yet, Paul was quick to add, "if you can get your freedom, grab the opportunity" (cf. 1 Corinthians 7:21). It was not only Paul who had a problem completely implementing his **principles** into completely just and righteous **pragmatics**. Consider the plight of the Church in America in **its** response to this verse during the slavery of Black people over 1000 years later. Instead of **transforming**, the Church **conformed** to the traditions and convictions of men; slavery was **all right**, and this view represented the consensus of the **majority** of churchmen of yesteryear. Today, we know from the clear light of God's Word that such servitude was morally wrong and a complete antithesis to the Spirit of God's admonition: "There is neither bond nor free."

As to the final and most controversial part of Galatians 3:28—"there is neither male nor female"—again, Paul the theologian and Paul the man of society come into conflict in terms of **practical** application; but if you take into account the historical context in which Paul the churchman had to implement his theology, you can be more understanding of **why** he wrote to Timothy as he did. Paul was, like every other person in the first century Christian Church, a child of his times, and in those days decent and respectable women might be **seen** in public, but never **heard** in public! Only loose and disreputable women would speak in public, and particularly in **mixed** company! Women were considered the chattle **property** of men; they had **no** rights, **no** voice, and **nothing** to offer their husbands but sexual companionship, housekeeping, and motherhood to **his** children! If women had **any** questions concerning events happening around them, they were directed to their **own** husbands; never to any other man! To do otherwise was to show great disrespect and bring shame to the name of their husbands or fathers. They had **no** opinions to offer and no advice or counsel to give; they were to speak **only** when spoken to, and even **then** in a tone of **submissiveness** that would not offend the authoritarian male image. Hence, Paul says, "Let the women learn in silence with all subjection. But I suffer not a woman to teach, nor to usurp authority over the man, but to be in silence" (1 Timothy 2:1 and 1 Timothy 2:11, 12). Among the higher class women of Paul's day, it was customary to even **veil the face** in public mixed company, to never walk **beside** but always **behind** the man, and **never** question his decisions, no matter **what** they were!

And yet, even this apparently strident statement of Paul against women, when examined, yields insights into the freedom of Christian women. For instance, what other secular writer in New Testament times even posited the idea that women should **learn alongside men**? Paul was way far ahead of the thinking of his day. Or, to examine Paul's statement a little further, Paul would not allow a man or a child or any Christian person to teach, unless that person had first **learned** the subject. The principle Paul expounds for women is applicable to all Christians.

Is it any wonder then, when those 120 men **and women** came down from the Upper Room, when the Day of Pentecost was fully come—filled with the Holy Ghost and speaking with other tongues, as the Spirit gave them utterance—that the multitude was all amazed hearing the wonderful works of God in their own tongues by both men **and women**!

The Scriptures say that others mocking said, "These men are full of new wine." Their behavior was so unusual; their breach of social graces so anti-social; imagine men **and women**—what a public spectacle! They **must** be drunken! But this was the Church in one of its purest forms—**every** member speaking the wonderful works of God; both men **and women**!

Many who oppose the prophetic role of women in the Church mistakenly equate the Women's Liberation Movement, the Equal Rights Amendment, and other political and social reform initiatives in modern society as the catalysts for the awakening of the Church's consciousness to the place of women in the Gospel Ministry. Nothing could be further from the truth! Indeed, the freedoms we claim as children of God antedate, transcend, and far surpass **any** philosophy of liberation that secular society could ever conceptualize. In fact, every liberty, freedom, and idea of equality in all human relationships had their genesis in the teachings of our faith; but what we are talking about is **far** above any

Where are the Scriptures?

of those things! Women's Liberation, E.R.A., and all other political and social reform initiatives are not even to be **compared** with the liberty in the Spirit and the freedom in Christ that we share as members of the Church. These movements in modern society are designed to bring equality of opportunity that does not get to the **heart** of the problem, because they do nothing to change the disposition of the human **heart**! They are **physical/social** in nature, and even when their goals **are** realized, the end results always fall far short of the freedoms sought and aspired for!

Definitely, these have no relationship to the higher callings of **spiritual dimensions** that are the focal point of our deliberations; for what they seek, **we already have, and much more**! For we know "if the Son therefore shall make you free, ye shall be free, indeed." Therefore, anyone who would use these human initiatives as an argument to try to take away from a Member of the Church the freedom that the Son of God has given to them is presenting a "Mickey Mouse" rationale that is completely devoid of validity and good common sense! Every Christian is not only free, but **free indeed**—free indeed to become **anything** the gifts of the Holy Spirit equip him or her to become, and that includes being a preacher, pastor, evangelist, teacher, interpreter, ruler, healer, giver, minister, miracle worker, etc., and no human being should in **any way** hinder the exercise of that freedom!

The Church would be utterly shocked to learn how many women through the years have been given the gifts of prophecy and exhortation, but were afraid to acknowledge their calling because of the strong opposition from their church, their pastor, their husband, their children, their families, other Christian women, and from the society of unbelievers. The tragedy represented by their great loss to the Kingdom of God can best be measured in the many souls who have already gone into a Christless eternity, and the countless numbers for which that same eternal destiny is just a matter of time! However, it also shows itself in the many frustrated women who cause their families untold sufferings because they secretly carry the burden of those spiritual gifts without ever exercising or using them; so they never have peace of mind or the contentment of heart that comes from the assurance of living in the center of God's will!

The tremendous revolution that would occur in our churches today to bring about a spiritual renaissance that would surpass our highest hopes to reach the lost before our Lord's return can still possibly come to pass; if **we** can just get out of the way and let the Holy Spirit use all of the available resources without our prejudicial traditions that would hinder. For by our traditions, we make null and void the Word of God!

There are **always** new facts to be learned in this life, new frontiers to be discovered, new challenges to be overcome, and nowhere is that truth more viable than in relation to the Word of God. We are **constantly** learning things from it **today** that we did not understand **yesterday** and, while they may be new to **us**, they are **not** new to God; for they were clearly presented in His Word **all the time**! We simply did not have eyes to see, ears to hear, or minds sufficiently disciplined by the Holy Spirit to understand!

So great is the mind and will of our God that the old is

forever new, and the new is forever old in His Word; because it is from everlasting to everlasting and so we are compelled to echo the words of Paul in Romans 11:33, 34:

> O the depth of the riches both of the wisdom and knowledge of God! How unsearchable are his judgments, and his ways past finding out. For who hath known the mind of the Lord or who hath been his counselor?

The Scriptures quoted in opposition to the ordination into the ministry applies only on a level of **physical/social** dimension, but what is at issue in this discussion must be addressed on a level of **spiritual** dimension! We are discussing **spiritual gifts** given by the Holy Spirit to do **spiritual battle** and to give **spiritual enablement** to the Church; all under the control and direction of the Holy Spirit **irrespective** of all physical differences for which He has no prejudicial regard, and so for the sake of winning lost souls, let the Lord of the harvest send laborers into His vineyard without our physical encumbrances and restraints, and spiritual victory will prevail!

The bottom line of the differences among us concerning the prophetic role of women finally boils down to the question: **Who is in charge of the Church**? Is it **God**, or is it **men** of God? Persons who seek to deny the right of women to be so used by the Holy Spirit seem to always want to transfer the burden of proof that He does to **those of us** who repose our faith in this matter implicitly in Him; but because He is **God all by Himself**,

God Cannot Will Not violate His own Word — so how has He Limited Himself is the ISSUE!

He does not **have** to be proven! Indeed, there is nothing more for us to say; for the Holy Spirit has never sought the counsels of men as to whom He will give His gifts, and He never will. So we are content to leave it **exclusively in His hands, and rest our case there**!

Whenever the traditionalists who are opposed to the ordination of women address themselves to Paul's message in Ephesians 5:21-23, they state that Paul gets down to the practical or the "nitty-gritty" things of life. The Christian Church **has** to be in complete agreement with everything Paul expresses in this passage, and there is no controversy on this point; for indeed, wives **are** to submit themselves to their own husbands, and the husband is the head of the wife. However, this fact is completely irrelevant to the spiritual gifts of prophecy and exhortation and has little to do with the aim of this book. The practical or nitty-gritty things of life are addressing the **physical/social relationships** between husbands and wives, and not the **spiritual ministries** of the Church! The only possible relationship that the one might have to do with the other is that learning subjection in the home of her husband can help equip a woman to more positively respond to the lessons of subjection to the Holy Spirit in the Church; now **that** conclusion has both validity and relevance. Yet, it is a conclusion which likewise is applicable to men. For the words of Ephesians 5:21 are a call for mutual submission, out of reverence for Christ, between husbands and wives. Wives **should** be subject to their own husbands, and husbands should be subject to their own wives. Moreover, **everyone**—both husbands and wives—must be subject to the Holy Spirit. (Ephesians 5:18).

Chapter 3

An Ancient Revolution in the Modern Pulpit

Whenever the traditionalists who are opposed to the ordination of women address themselves to Paul's message in Ephesians 5:21-23, they state that Paul gets down to the practical or the "nitty-gritty" things of life. The Christian Church **has** to be in complete agreement with everything Paul expresses in this passage, and there is no controversy on this point; for indeed, wives **are** to submit themselves to their own husbands, and the husband is the head of the wife. However, this fact is completely irrelevant to the spiritual gifts of prophecy and exhortation and has little to do with the aim of this book. The practical or nitty-gritty things of life are addressing the **physical/social relationships** between husbands and wives, and not the **spiritual ministries** of the Church! The only possible relationship that the one might have to do with the other is that learning subjection in the home of her husband can help equip a woman to more positively respond to the lessons of subjection to the Holy Spirit in the Church; now **that** conclusion has both validity and relevance. Wives **should** be subject to their own husbands, and **everyone**—both husbands and wives—must be subject to the Holy Spirit.

The tradition against the ordination of women often argues that it would make God the Author of confusion to command a woman to be subject to her husband and at the same time place her as a **ruler** over the flock of God. Well, the Lord **is not** nor can He **ever be** the Author of confusion; but this is precisely what He would **become** if He allowed **any human being**, male **or** female, to be a **ruler** over the flock of God! The Church of Jesus Christ does indeed have a Ruler, but He is the Holy Spirit, and **not** the pastor or preacher. Pastors and preachers are **ministers** of God, and the word "**minister**" means "**servant**"; they are, in fact, **servants** that are called **by** and responsible **to** the Ruler—the **Holy Spirit**! It is **extremely unfortunate** that so many pastors and preachers view the position of the minister as a ruler of the church and do not understand that the nature of their calling is to **serve** and not to **rule**! They are to be as their Lord was in His earthly ministry: "Not to be ministered unto; but to minister," and that is why they are designated by the label "minister." Indeed, a man **should** rule over his house; but not the **Church**! He is commanded by the Word to "Take **care** of the church of God" (1 Timothy 3:5). Let it be repeated again and again: ministers are to take care of the church of God, not **rule** over it! He is but a servant and steward over that which belongs to

Someone **Else**, and **only** the **Owner** has a right to **rule** over it! The Owner (Christ) has sent the Holy Spirit **to take His place** as Ruler, and anyone with the most basic theological training can understand this truth with no problem at all and not confuse the issue by putting mere, unworthy human beings into the picture; for they certainly don't belong **anywhere** in the rulership of the Church of Christ.

The tradition which opposes the ordination of women often uses Paul's quotation of the Corinthian slogan concerning women keeping silence in the church "as also saith the law." As demonstrated previously, these words are definitely a perversion of the Word of God. Even though **we** believe that all Scripture is inspired by God and written for our admonition, it must be remembered that everything that is said **in** the Word of God was not necessarily spoken **by** God, and the so-called "law" commanding women to keep silence in the Church is one of such statements! This command was surely **not** part of the **Moral Law** spoken by **God to man**. It probably was part of the **Ceremonial Law** spoken by **man** to **man** as part of their **traditions** in the disciplines of worship. Well might the Corinthian males have said, "Women shall sit in a section of the church segregated from men as also saith the law," for this was the tradition in discipline of worship in all of the Jewish temple and synagogue worship settings, and for that matter it is still true today in Orthodox Jewish worship settings. A little scholarship, research, and academic discipline in Biblical theology would help all of us to better understand the differences between the Moral Law that was spoken by God and the Ceremonial Laws that represent the "traditions of the elders" that are not really **God's** commandments! As a point of fact, the student of Scripture searches the Old Testament in vain for any semblance of a direct statement commanding women to be silent and to only learn from their husbands at home. In all candor, it must be said that listening to human beings will always mislead you, even concerning the words recorded in the Bible. While I am being candid, some basic exposure to the study of Greek and Hebrew would significantly help our brothers and sisters in the Gospel Ministry to better understand the Word of God in the finer shades of meaning of the words that are spoken in it. To illustrate the handicap they must labor under without such exposure—our English language has three tenses while the Greek has seven, and so they miss so **much** in their understanding of the Bible. It is necessary to remind our readers of the tremendous revolution that would occur in our churches today to bring about spiritual renaissance that would surpass our highest hopes to reach the lost before our Lord's return. If we can just get out of the way, and let the Holy Spirit use all of the available resources without our traditional restraints on them.

These traditional restraints are not the work of **evil** men, but of **sincere** Christians who feel they are defenders of the faith who "earnestly counted for the faith which was once delivered unto the saints" (Jude 3b). They are considered persons of **strong "convictions"** in this matter; in fact, that is one of their favorite words in describing their opposition to women sharing the spiritual gifts of prophecy and exhortation. It is a **"principle of conviction"** with them, they say! However, it must be said that so-called "convictions" that are born out of ignorance of **God's** will and of **God's** way, as revealed biblically, can be even **more** detrimental **within** the Body of Christ than the opposition from the enemy without!

To contend with those **within** the church who have the zeal of God but not according to knowledge is a tremendously traumatic challenge for the Fellowship of God's people to overcome! The Apostle Paul would, in pathos, cry out in agony of spirit concerning this controversy surrounding women members in the Body of Christ: "Brethren, my heart's desire and prayer to God for the (Church) is that they might (have understanding of the sovereignty of God). For I bear them record that they have a zeal of God; but not according to knowledge. For they being ignorant of God's (sovereignty), and going about to establish their own (sovereignty); have not submitted themselves unto the (sovereignty) of God" (to make a paraphrasable application of Romans 10:1-3). Indeed, who could speak better to this issue than the Apostle Paul; for before his understanding was opened to God's sovereignty, as Saul of Tarsus—a man of very strong convictions—he **persecuted** the Church of Jesus Christ. He was **thoroughly** convinced he was **right** and that he was actually doing God a great **service** by putting down the heretical "Way," and he was convinced by his strong **convictions** that he had to "earnestly contend for the faith which was once delivered unto the (elders)," and that meant total annihilation of the Christian community and all of its members! Thanks be to God, Paul learned the truth and was greatly used by the Holy Spirit to perpetuate the very Gospel he once sought to destroy. In the not too distant future, enlightenment will come to many church members who oppose the Spirit of God bestowing upon women the spiritual gifts of prophecy and exhortation, and they will wonder why we ever made such a problem for ourselves in the first place; for nothing is impossible with God!

The convictions of a person's conscience do not indicate what is right or what is wrong. They only call a person to adhere to what he **thinks** is right and to shun what he **thinks** is wrong. The Apostle Peter had convictions when, in the process of receiving a vision from God who told him to "Rise, Peter: kill, and eat," he told the Lord: "Not so, Lord; for I have never eaten anything that is common or unclean." To which the Lord responded, **"What God hath cleansed, that call not thou common"** (Acts 10:13ff.). The convictions of Peter's conscience led him to shun the will of God to evangelize Gentiles and to actually tell His Lord, "No." Peter's convictions were not based on the Word and truth of God Who had cleansed all people, thus preparing them for the Gospel. Peter's convictions were wrong, God was right. So Peter had to change and bring his convictions into conformity with the will of God. Eventually, after experiencing all kinds of miracles, Peter said: "God hath shewed me that I should not call any man common or unclean" (Acts 10:28).

The fact that the tradition opposing the ordination of women questions how **far** the admonition for women to keep silence in the churches should extend is very interesting; for if they really believe this is a commandment of **God**, then they should already know that such a command would be **all-inclusive** and extend **all the way** because the commandments of God are absolutely complete! Our response to this uncertainty of how **far** to extend the silence of women in the church that is consistent with their own convictions would be not to stop with the pastor, preacher, or teacher; but go **all** the way to **every speaking position** held by women! Indeed, they should practice what they preach, and that means no women singers in the choirs, no women presidents, secretaries, teachers, directors, superintendents, missionaries, or any other position of service wherein the rule of silence is broken—**beginning** where they serve as pastor and upholder of tradition.

There is, indeed, a consistent teaching of the subjection of a woman unto a man in their **social** relationships as husband and wife in the **home**; but our deliberations concerning women sharing the spiritual gifts of prophecy and exhortation deals with **spiritual** relationships within the Body of Christ, and such physical restraints have no relevance in it, or even in our discussion of it!

If we sound unusually harsh against the traditionalists and all persons who share their ideas, it is not out of ill will but out of genuine love and concern. Indeed, our hearts go out to them in sincerest compassion; for they suffer acutely from presumption, and it must be a tremendous burden for them to carry—having to make the weighty decision of presuming whom the Holy Spirit has "called" and whom He has "not called," given the limited knowledge and understanding we human beings have at our disposal! Men who have to separate the saved from the lost, the "went" from the "sent," the wheat from the tares, the "called" from the "not called," the right from the wrong have assumed to themselves a responsibility that only an omnipotent, omnipresent, and omniscient

God can handle, and they are to be loved and prayed for in the spirit of patience!

We happily join the ranks of those who leave such a great responsibility **completely** and **exclusively** in the hands of the Holy Spirit; for it is **His** Church, not ours, and so it is **His** problem, not ours! Our problem is to faithfully serve "**our** calling to fulfill," and we are thankful that this is **all** the Spirit of God asks of us, because it is **enough** of a challenge to last us an entire lifetime!

Joyfully, we can proclaim in full assurance that women can share, without any **human** restraints, the wonders of God's grace, mercy, and love that He bestows on **all** of His children irrespective of their physical differences; even if a great number of my colleagues in the ministry cannot appreciate that fact! It is unfortunate that they refuse to use their minds, not thinking **through** what they are doing, and continue to blindly follow the foolish traditions of men that deny the Holy Spirit His sovereignty as God. In light of this reality, all of God's children—whether young or old, male or female, black or white, educated or uneducated, rich or poor, or any other category that reflects our physical/social differences—all would do well to appropriate to their hearts and lives the truths of God recorded in 1 Corinthians 2:9-16:

> But as it is written, eye hath not seen, nor ear heard, neither have entered into the heart of man, the things which God hath prepared for them that love him. But God hath revealed them unto us by his spirit; for the spirit searcheth all things, yea, the deep things of God. For what man knoweth the things of a man, save the

spirit of man which is in him? Even so the things of God knoweth no man, but the spirit of God. Now we have received, not the spirit of the world, but the spirit which is of God: That we might know the things that are freely given to us of God. Which things also we speak, not in the words which man's wisdom teacheth, but which the Holy Ghost teacheth; **comparing spiritual things with spiritual.** But natural man receiveth not the things of the spirit of God: For they are foolishness unto him: Neither can he know them, because they are spiritually discerned. But he that is spiritual judgeth all things, yet he himself is judged of no man. For who hath known the mind of the Lord, that he may instruct him? But we have the mind of Christ.

Many compare the **spiritual** realities with the **physical/social** in the quest for a resolution of the problem with women ministers. Unfortunately, they again arrive at the wrong answers and conclusions in trying to solve this problem of women in possession of the spiritual gifts of prophecy and exhortation because such comparisons are never valid; for there is no significant **relativity** between the physical/social and the spiritual within the dimensions of **spiritual absolutes**!

There are **no**, I repeat **no**, specific verses in the Bible that clearly forbid women preachers; for the Holy Ghost would **not** nor could He contradict Himself; and so He **has** and He **is** distributing the gifts of prophecy and exhortation to **whomever He will**, and that includes **women** as well as men; for as the Third Person of the

Godhead, He too is **absolutely** no respecter of persons! (cf. 1 Corinthians 12:11)

Indeed, the tradition opposed to the ordination of women in all honesty cannot overlook the fact that there are instances throughout the Scriptures where references are made to women who were prophetesses, and when you find them speaking and teaching the Word of the Lord to His people that includes **all** the men, women, boys, and girls that make up the number of **His** people! God did not have His **prophets** speak only to **men**, or His **prophetesses** speak only to **women**! When He anointed a messenger to speak for Him, the message was to **all of His people**, and as it was true yesterday it is true today, and it will be true tomorrow; for God does **not** change! These messengers were limited only insofar as they served **their** day in doing what God wanted them to do, and there were **no** limitations in their sphere of activity in the accomplishment of the God-given tasks and assignments. They were **His** prophets and prophetesses, and the Bible does not record **everything** they did and said; but **whatever** they did, it must have been important enough to God for Him to call them out from among the masses to do His will! Surely, Miriam did **more** than just lead the women in singing after the great victory over Pharaoh; but if that is all the Lord recorded, **so be it**! Deborah the prophetess did much **more** than deal on a one-to-one basis with Barak; the Scriptures say, "and Deborah, a prophetess, the wife of Lapidoth, she **judged** Israel at that time" (Judges 4:4). Like the Prophet Samuel after her, she was God's messenger **and** administrator; for they were **both** prophets and judges! Anna the prophetess "was of a great age" and the Scriptures say that she "departed not from the temple, but served God with fastings and prayers night and day." Because of her advanced age, her ministry was confined to the temple; but obviously, the many years she served there afforded her many opportunities to exercise her prophetic ministry among thousands of worshipers. However, we do have a record of the content of at least **one** of her messages, and it is recorded for us in Luke 2:38: "And she coming in that instant **gave thanks** likewise unto the Lord, **and spake of him** to all them that looked for redemption in Jerusalem."

Nowhere in the Scriptures are there any claims of a prophetic role for the Virgin Mary, the Mother of Jesus, and I have never heard of **anyone** attributing such a role to her until a traditionalist projected it as an alleged argument by advocates of women in the ministry. If anyone is guilty of using such an argument, their argument is not just **weak**, it is **utterly untrue**! Nor is it true that the women at the tomb of Jesus are accorded the gift of prophecy and exhortation; for they were simply relaying the reminder of Jesus' promise to meet His disciples in Galilee following His resurrection.

However, on the Day of Pentecost, women **were** there in the Upper Room with men, and they **all** there were **speaking**, as the Bible says concerning **all** those present: "And there appeared unto them cloven tongues like as of fire, and it sat upon **each** of them. And they were **all** filled with the Holy Ghost, and began to **speak** with other tongues, as the spirit gave them utterance" (Acts 2:3-4). They were **all** filled, and they **all spoke**! In fact, one of the reasons "others mocking, said, These men are full of new wine" was because **all 120 of them** spoke the "wonderful works of God" in the language of all the many different nations of people gathered at Jerusalem! To be sure, it was Peter, speaking for **all 120** of the Church members who responded to the accusation of drunkenness by quoting Joel 2:28-29, but Peter was explaining the message and actions of both the men **and the women**; for Joel speaks of sons **and daughters** prophesying; of servants **and handmaidens** prophesying!

We are clearly instructed in this matter when men must countenance Acts 2:17-18; for this message from God cuts through **all** the rhetoric, interpretations, opinions, and convictions of men; so we can hear **the Word of the Lord**! In this particular Scripture passage, **God says**—not Peter, James, or John; not Paul, Luke, or Matthew; but **God Himself speaks**:

> And it shall come to pass in the last days, **saith God**, I will pour out of my spirit upon **all** flesh: And your sons and your **daughters** shall prophesy, and your young men shall see visions, and your old men shall dream dreams: and on my servants and on my **handmaidens** I will pour out in those days of my spirit; and they **shall prophesy**.

The tradition opposing the ordination of women says the matter of prophecy in the Old and New Testament is unclear and uncertain with respect to women, and that there is no instance of women ever doing **any** prophecy or teaching where men were or as the men did in the Old or the New Testaments. These two statements are not only **contradictory**, they are also very **wrong**! There is **nothing** unclear **or** uncertain concerning the prophetic role of women in the Old **or** New Testaments; for like their male counterparts, they served their age in doing the will of God, and then passed off the scene. The tradition opposing the ordination of women cites an instance of a woman, Deborah, prophesying and teaching and significantly contributing to the leadership of God's people as a prophetess and judge to **all** the people of Israel—both **men** and women! Even this tradition admits that Deborah "told Barak what the Lord had said," and this is precisely **all** prophets do—they tell people what the **Lord** has said! It is **God's** message, not **theirs**, and they are **God's** servants, and not their own!

With respect to Peter's miraculous deliverance from prison, Acts 12:5 says, "Peter therefore was kept in prison: but prayer was made **without ceasing** of **the church** unto God for him." "When Peter came out of prison, he went to John Mark's house where the **Church** was gathered for prayer." It was **not** a "woman's prayer meeting" where "no men were there at all." On the contrary, it was **the Church** at prayer, and since they were having all day and all night prayer meetings—for the Bible says, "prayer was made without ceasing"—not only women, but probably men, women, **and children** were present at this important church prayer meeting when Peter knocked at the door! The Living Bible translates Peter's words in Acts 12:17: "He motioned for them to quiet down, and told them what had happened, and how the Lord had brought him out of jail. 'Tell James and the others what happened,' he said—and left for safer quarters." As all through the Bible, the word "brethren" (cf. KJV) is overwhelmingly used generically and does not denote just the male sex exclusively!

Traditionalists trying to explain away Philip's four daughters who were prophetesses say, "You read about Philip the Evangelist who had four daughters who prophesied, but we never read about any prophecy they made in public." The traditionalist admits there have been prophetesses who prophesied; but simply because **we** never read about any prophesies they made in public does not mean that they **didn't** make any! The Living Bible says, "Philip had four unmarried daughters who had the gift of prophecy" (Acts 21:9). Surely, the Holy Spirit would not give them the **gift**—as He says in His Word, "And the same man (Philip) had four daughters, virgins, **which did prophesy**!"—and they did **not** exercise their gift to the people at Caesarea; that would not make any sense! It could very well be true that they **did** prophesy to Paul not to go to Jerusalem just as the believers in Tyre had done, and perhaps the Holy Spirit dispatched Agabus from the Mother Church at Jerusalem to confirm both the prophesies he had received in Tyre and Caesarea; but Paul did not listen to **any** of them, **including** Agabus, and thus, as a matter of probability, disobeyed the Holy Ghost! (However, see Acts 20:22-23; 19:21.)

Finally, traditionalists say, in the absence of Scripture or any information from beginning to end of women speaking or preaching, it's difficult to understand how many would seek to maintain that women have a call to preach. It would be **more** fair to say that many who believe that women **do** have a call to preach could very well base their argument on the many testimonies and Scripture accounts that were cited by the traditionalists' statements in this section **alone**, as reason enough not only to **believe** it, but to significantly **strengthen** that belief!

It will **always** be difficult for men to understand that "which the Holy Ghost teacheth; comparing spiritual things with spiritual" as long as they continue to compare **spiritual** with **physical/social**!

The gifts of prophecy and exhortation are **spiritual gifts** that are given by the Holy Spirit to the spiritually-minded servants of God, and to appreciate the Giver, the receivers and what those gifts contribute to the work of the Kingdom of God must be **spiritually discerned**.

How grateful many of us are because the Holy Spirit has given us enough spiritual discernment to entrust to Him the right to share His gifts with **whomever** He chooses, and we can do it with full assurance that He knows what is best for His Church!

Allow me, in light of that assurance, to respectfully submit to all traditionalists who have believed and taught that women could **not** share with men the spiritual gifts of prophecy and exhortation that we **admit we have been wrong!** Indeed, we have been the victims of those who were **themselves** victimized by inadequate training in the Word and limited exposures to the theological discipline that would have taught us better. It could have been clear to us a **long time ago**, and would have saved us a lot of controversy and mental anguish if only someone, somewhere, had simply shared the **whole counsel of God** with us on this subject. Then the fulfillment of God's prophecy in Acts 2:17-18 could have **already** found fulfillment in all of our many local congregations, and more souls would have been saved because more Gospel would have been preached! Thank God, it is not too late to explain to people everywhere that we were following what we considered a **time-honored tradition** that had convinced us with strong convictions that we were right! Now that it has been made clear, we are willing to admit, **we were wrong!** It is not the **first** time we have had to change our thoughts and ways to coincide with the thoughts and ways of God, and unfortunately it probably won't be the **last** time such an adjustment and change on **our part** will be necessary. However, we are ready to let the world know of our willingness to turn the calling of preachers of the Gospel of Jesus Christ over completely and exclusively into the hands of the Holy Spirit, to use as He sees fit, and leave the results to Him! Amen!

Chapter 4

The Scriptures Answer The Critics

Clarity necessitates the repetition of basic spiritual truths already covered in previous explanations; but because of the gravity of the ultimately eternal consequences resulting in the perpetuation of the ungodly tradition of denying the Holy Spirit His sovereignty in the distribution of spiritual gifts, perhaps even redundancy for the sake of emphasizing the **truth**, is quite in order.

To begin with, we must never lose sight of the **bottom line** of this issue—cutting through the rhetoric, misinterpretations, opinions, and convictions of men—and hear the **Word of the Lord**. **God** says, not Peter, James, John, Paul, Luke, or any of the other **Apostles**; not what denominations, conventions, adjudicatories, associations, councils of churches, individual congregations, or pastors say; but **God** says:

> In the last days, I will pour out of my spirit upon **all** flesh; and your sons **and your daughters** shall

> prophesy, and your young men shall see visions, and your old men shall dream dreams. And on **my** servants and on **my handmaidens** I will pour out in those days of my spirit, **and they shall prophesy** (Acts 2:17-18).

The clear and unmistakable prophecy of Joel was fulfilled, beginning at Pentecost when **all 120 of them** were **all** filled with the Holy Ghost! "And it shall come to pass in the last days, saith God" (Acts 2:17a).

We have heard a **thousand times over** what **men** have said; now hear the Word of the **Lord**! There really is nothing more to discuss, interpret, or deliberate on—God said it, and that settles it! Good for any of us, if we believe it.

That's **tough** if God's Word runs contrary to our traditions and opinions; it's **too bad** if our interpretations of Scripture are in antithesis to **His** will and **His** way; tough for **us**, and too bad for **us**. God says, "My ways are not your ways; neither my thoughts your thoughts: as the heavens are higher than the earth; so are my ways over your ways" (Isaiah 55:8).

So, dear reader, whether you side with those who say that the Holy Spirit **cannot** and does **not** give to women the spiritual gifts of prophecy and exhortation; or whether you side with those who say that He **does** give to women as **well** as men the spiritual gifts of prophecy and exhortation—**neither** side makes **any difference**! The Body of Christ is a **theocracy**, and **not** a democracy; so whether we cast our vote **for or against** women in the Gospel Ministry, the matter is **not** decided by **us**; but **exclusively** by the **Holy Spirit**, and Him **alone**! He seeks

no counsel from apostles, pastors, evangelists, deacons, trustees, or any **other** member of the Church. The spiritual gifts are His **alone** to give, and He gives them to whomever **He** wills; therefore, humans have **absolutely nothing** to say about it! Indeed, I would like to close my response with this statement of that fact; but lest we be accused of evading the traditionalists' arguments let us prayerfully consider them in turn:

To begin with, our traditionalist quotes 1 Timothy 2:11-14:

> Let the woman learn in silence with all subjection. But I suffer not a woman to teach, nor to usurp authority over the man, but to be in silence. For Adam was first formed, then Eve. And Adam was not deceived, but the woman being deceived was in the transgression. Notwithstanding she shall be saved in childbearing, if they continue in faith and charity and holiness with sobriety.

All of us would agree that Paul's advice to women to listen and learn quietly, humbly and under subjection is excellent advice; but that advice could well apply not **only** to women, but to men and children as well. Indeed, **everyone** would do well to listen and learn quietly, humbly and under subjection in all of life's situations. And only then to teach. To be sure **no** one should usurp authority that belongs to someone else; for the word "usurp" means to seize or to take hold by force or without right that which belongs to someone else. Paul knew there were those kinds of women, even in the fellowship of the Church, who would do **precisely** that, and he emphatically warns against that kind of ungodly behavior. Parenthetically, it should be noted that the most effective learning process **necessitates** listening quietly and humbly and under subjection to the **teacher**, and in Paul's case that meant **women** listening quietly and humbly and under subjection to **men**, because in the very next verse he explains that **he** suffers not a woman to teach! Notice Paul says, "**But** I suffer not a woman to teach"; he does **not** say, "I suffer not a woman to teach"; no, he says, "**But** I suffer not a woman to teach." The word "but" is significant in that Paul's ministry was more among the Gentiles, and their most recent deliverance from paganism needed to be as clean and clear-cut as possible. Many of those pagan religions had female deities, goddesses or temple worships wherein women played a prominent role as priestesses and teachers: Ashtoreth, Diana, Venus, Aphrodite, and Ashtartu just to name a few. They were all terribly licentuous, carnal and sexual; fertile in nature, sensuous in character, and very strong in their appeal to the natural man (or woman). As you have already surmised, women were greatly used in the teaching services of these pagan religions. As a reaction to these strong pagan influences, Paul realized that the Christian Church had to be **extremely** careful in its formative years and steer clear of **anything** that might even **faintly** resemble the pagan traditions from which the Gentiles had been delivered through their new life in Christ Jesus. So not encouraging the use of women in the teaching ministry may have served a very useful purpose in keeping the Christian community a distinct and separated people. Here Paul was applying the theology of Christian freedom to his cultural context. The principle was one of expedience and edification. If eating meat would cause his brother to stumble, Paul would never eat meat in his brother's presence (cf. 1 Corinthians 8:13; Acts 15:19ff.). When the early Church came into contact with their society, they restrained their Christian freedom which promoted the equality of women with men. However, inside the private inner circles of her fellowship, her *koinonia*, the Church laid aside the traditions and ethics of men exclusively and allowed the Spirit of God and the Word of Jesus to have its way totally.

Now, for our generation **today**, identification with that facet of paganism is no longer a real problem to the Church; but we **do** have a serious problem, and it is a problem characteristic of the "last days" or Laodicean Church Age: a Church wherein women outnumber the men in attendance and availability for service as teachers. The Word of the Lord **must** be taught in the latter days just as it has been taught in the former days, and if **men** are not serviceable because of their unbelief or unavailability, then it is **more** than highly conceivable that more and more the Holy Spirit will be calling upon the service of women to the ministry of "**teaching** them to observe all things whatsoever I have commanded you."

It should also be noted that Paul says, "But **I** suffer not a woman to teach." He is not speaking absolutely, but temporarily. The tense of the Greek verb used indicates "I do not *at this time* permit a woman to teach." At the time in question the Church at Ephesus was under the siege of false teachers (cf. 1 Timothy 1:3-4, 6-7, 19-20; 4:1; 2 Timothy 1:15; 4:14-15; 2:16-18). In order to correct the situation Timothy was to strictly limit the teaching ministry of the Church by choosing the most competent and qualified teachers. The prohibition against women being teachers would eventually be lifted, just as Eve would be vindicated from the deception of the serpent (1 Timothy 2:15). Thus, what appears to be a strident statement by Paul in plain antithesis to the freedom of women in the Church turns out, under closer examination, to be a drastic procedure to preserve the Church from full-scale apostasy.

There is **no** place recorded in Scripture wherein the Holy Spirit says that **He** will not bestow upon women the spiritual gift of teaching! On the contrary, looking in all of our churches you will observe **more** women than men being **used** by the Holy Spirit in the ministry of teaching, and He is honoring their teaching efforts by enlightening His people concerning His will and His way through this ministry. Again, I challenge everyone who shares the viewpoint of the tradition opposing women's ordination to practice what you preach; uphold your own convictions and immediately cease and desist from allowing women to teach anywhere in the church where **you** fellowship; for according to **you**, they should not break the rule of silence in the Church by teaching **anything** or **anyone** in the Fellowship!

Again, many traditionalists state that a woman, because of her nature and make-up, is more susceptible to deception and this disqualifies her for positions of leadership and guardianship over the doctrines and truths once delivered unto the saints. On the contrary, the Bible teaches that **all** human beings whether male or female share a common heritage of susceptibility to deception. Indeed, in Jeremiah 17:9 we read: "The heart is deceitful above all things, and desperately wicked: who can know it?" The Bible also says, "For **all** have sinned, and come short of the glory of God" (Romans 3:23). Our susceptibility to deception is not based on **sex**, but on our fallen nature and conscious and unconscious perverseness to do evil! Persons who talk in broad generalities, in stereotypical fashion, and who label groups of people into prejudicial categories display very little scholarship and sensitivity to the truth, and would do well not to publicly display their lack of understanding of the truth.

The traditionalists opposing the ordination of women like to quote 1 Timothy 2: "Adam was first formed, then Eve" (1 Timothy 2:13). So their analysis of verse 14 is interesting; they say the Bible makes it clear that Eve was totally deceived. Adam went in with his eyes wide open. Indeed, this analysis is interesting because it puts Adam in a worse light than Eve, and I'm sure that was not the intent of the traditionalists; after all, Eve was totally deceived by the great deceiver **himself**, Satan, that evil one, and **no** human is any match for him! Genesis 3:6 says, "And the women saw that the tree was good for food, and that it was pleasant to the eyes, and a tree to be desired to make one wise, she took of the fruit thereof, and did eat, and gave also unto her husband **with her**: and he did eat." The question might well be posed: Eve was deceived by Satan, but what was **Adam's** excuse? When questioned by God concerning this, Adam blamed Eve, and Eve blamed the serpent; so God cursed the serpent, but He also pronounced judgment on **both** Adam and Eve; for **both were without excuse**! **Both** Adam and Eve knew the eternal consequences of disobedience to God's command, so one was no better or worse than the other!

Finally, we are constantly reminded by traditionalists

that a bishop must be "the husband of one wife" and not the wife of one husband; it therefore becomes necessary to explain that the intent of this prerequisite was to address the problem of Christian ministers, pastors, or bishops following the traditions of the pagan priesthood wherein they had sexual relations with every woman they could who came to the temple for worship rites; in fact, in some pagan cultures, sexual relations between female worshipers and male priests was part of the worship ritual. It would have been extremely easy to bring into the infant Christian Church this practice or some modification of it and destroy the very moral fabric of the Christian fellowship before it had a chance to develop sufficiently to overcome this onslaught of the evil one!

Supposing the Christian Church would impose a literal interpretation of this requirement, not just as it relates to women, but to everyone. What would happen to the Church's supply of boy preachers? Men like Dr. R. Wendell Phillips and Dr. P. S. Wilkinson, just to name two great preachers of this generation who started out as boy preachers, would never have made it because they were not "the husband of one wife." What of all the **bachelor ministers** whom the Holy Spirit has called to preach who have never been married and are not "the husband of one wife," and what of all the **widowers** who have outlived their wives and are not "the husband of one wife"? You can see why the literal interpretation of this passage of Scripture is so ridiculous and is only applied literally when denying women the exercise of their spiritual gifts of prophecy and exhortation!

While we have set forth to respond to the contentions presented by traditionalists, let it be understood that their contentions and my responses or any other arguments, concepts, interpretations, or convictions that represent the thinking of human mentalities in these deliberations have **no bearing whatsoever** on the Holy Spirit's sovereignty to do what **He** wills to do in this matter under discussion. What **we** must learn to say, and really mean it from our hearts, is: **"Have thine own way, Lord; have thine own way!**

Chapter 5

No Respecter of Persons

> Then Peter opened his mouth, and said, of a truth I perceive that God is no respecter of persons. But in every nation he that feareth him, and worketh righteousness, is accepted with him. (Acts 10:34, 35)

There is absolutely no need for **anyone** to take these two verses out of context for **any** reason; for they **adequately** say what they **mean**, and **positively** mean what **they say**—God **is** no respecter of persons! To be sure, Peter was specifically dealing with the prejudice that Jewish Christians had in fully accepting the **equality** of Gentile Christians; for it was an established **time-honored tradition** for Jews to believe, with the strongest **convictions**, that people of other nations could **not** share with them the blessings of salvation and the accompanying indwelling of the Holy Spirit. It was a surprise to Peter and his Jewish companions to learn that God loves **all people** that accept the salvation He has provided in

Christ; that Christ died for **all people** who believe in Him as their personal Saviour; that the Holy Spirit will give witness of His indwelling presence in the hearts and lives of **all people** who receive Christ Jesus as their Lord; so "that through his name **whosoever** believeth in him shall receive remission of sins" (Acts 10:43b). So it is written: "And they of the circumcision which believed were astonished, as many as came with Peter, because that on the Gentiles also was poured out the gift of the Holy Ghost" (Acts 10:45).

Later, when Peter was called into question about his ministry to the Gentiles by the Mother Church at Jerusalem, he said of Cornelius: "And he shewed us how he had seen an angel in his house, which stood and said unto him: send men to Joppa, and call for Simon, whose surname is Peter; who shall tell thee words whereby thou and **all thy house** shall be saved, and as I began to speak, the Holy Ghost fell on **them**, as on **us** at the beginning" (Acts 11:13-15). "At the beginning" refers to Pentecost, as recorded in Acts 2, and those who use this passage of Scripture in Acts 10 to substantiate the fact that God operates His Kingdom above **all human prejudices** are simply correlating these two passages as did Peter in Acts 11. Indeed, God is no respecter of persons, and like **every truth** concerning His personality, attributes, and character, this fact is **not relative**, but **absolute**! Well might it be said that God is **absolutely** no respecter of persons, and this applies to **every** area of human experience; it is a fact that is **absolute** and not **relative**. You cannot say that He is **no** respecter of persons in relation to **this**, but He **is** a respecter of persons in relation to **that**—that's **human relativity**, and human relativity has **no** place in a discussion of God's will and way. If God is no respecter of persons **here**, then He is also no respecter of persons over **there**. He is eternal, immutable, and unchanging in **every way** and in **everything**. That is because He is God all by Himself! This means if He is no respecter of persons as it concerns **race**, then He is no respecter of persons as it concerns **sex**. If He is no respecter of persons as it concerns the **color** of a person's **skin**, then He is no respecter of persons as it concerns whether the persons are rich or poor, etc. **All** of the **physical** differences (except those physical practices and differences which are the result of human perversity, such as homosexuality and the results of gender-changing surgery) that make us prejudiced against each other are not God's fault, but ours! Racial, sexual, geographical, cultural, and religious differences are **human** problems; God's will and way **transcend** them, so we are **not** saying that women can preach like **men**, but we **are** saying that women can preach like **women**!

Therefore, it is **not necessary** to rip Acts 2, Acts 10, or Acts 11 out of context to prove that God is no respecter of persons; for that **fact** runs through the complete fabric of the entire Bible, and that He calls women to preach as well as men is simply based on the **absoluteness** of that **fact**; no matter **where** you find it in the Scriptures!

The Apostle Paul expands again on this fact with specific delineations, and addresses **every** area of our **physical** differences in Galatians 3:28 wherein he says, "There is neither Jew nor Greek, there is neither bond nor free, there is neither male nor female; for ye are all one in Christ Jesus." Those of us who believe that the Holy

Spirit imparts the gifts of prophecy and exhortation to women as well as men, because He is no respecter of persons, do **not** believe that Galatians 3:28 eliminates or eradicates sexual differences; on the contrary, we believe being in Christ Jesus **enhances** this physical distinction, and we rejoice in it! Our oneness in Christ magnifies this physical distinction to the highest point of dignity that enables us to discern the **spiritual equality** of the sexes; so that **spiritual privileges** are accorded **both** sexes as the **Holy Spirit** sees fit to bestow them, and this fact presents no problem at all for us!

No matter what your background or sex is, in Christ we are all one, even though we are not all the same. The way is open to everybody. No woman believes that when she becomes a Christian, she is **no longer** a woman; indeed, the text in Galatians 3:28 does **not** say **that**; nor does it say, in Christ there is no son and no daughter; no mother or father, no husband or wife; nor is there a negation of **any** of these **physical** relationships. In fact, **all** of these relationships are enriched and enhanced for those who are "in Christ Jesus"! Children must **always** obey their parents as God has commanded; but this truth has **nothing** to do with the calling of preachers by the Holy Spirit any more than the physical relationships we share as husbands and wives, mothers and fathers, sisters and brothers.

Up until recent years, whenever we were confronted by the spiritual realities of women receiving from the Holy Spirit the gifts of prophecy and exhortation and going forth as Gospel ministers, we immediately wrote them off as forward, fanatical women with heretical ideas; trying to be men, instead of staying in the place of women, attempting to invade an area of Christian service that was reserved **exclusively** for men **only**! Women ministers were against our **traditions**; they had no business preaching the Gospel; they did not belong in the pulpit; we simply could **not** accept the fact that the Holy Spirit would even **call** a woman to preach the Gospel of Jesus Christ, and we were **convinced** it was **wrong, wrong, wrong** and our unbiblical convictions against it happening in our local congregations were **strong, strong, strong**! That's the way it **was**, and that's the way we felt it should **remain**!

By our tradition we trample underfoot the **sovereignty of God** in denying His absolute authority to dispense His spiritual gifts as **He** wills! Secondly, by our tradition we fail because we have an infinitesimal understanding of the dichotomy between the **spiritual** and **physical** realities of human existence, and like Nicodemus, we must be told over and over again, "That which is flesh is flesh, and that which is spirit is spirit." Thirdly, by our tradition we fail because we blindly perpetuate a tradition of men that was conceived in a misunderstanding of God's will and way—His personality, attributes, and character! Finally, by our tradition we fail because our collective experience represents a basic lack of biblical scholarship and exposure to theological disciplines that would give enablement to "**rightly** divide the word of truth"!

Let us again respectfully submit to all who have believed and taught that women could **not** share with men the spiritual gifts of prophecy and exhortation that we admit **we have been wrong**!

There is no need for us to continue to be stubborn in our attitudes on this subject; for convictions born of a lack of understanding result in **wrong convictions**, and they are not worthy of the energy and effort that must be put forth to defend them. Indeed, when something is wrong it is simply **wrong**, and just because we always had convictions that it was right does not in any way change its **wrongness**! Again, we are called upon to renounce this false teaching as we finally realize we have been the victims of the traditions of those who were **themselves** victimized by inadequate training in the Word, and by limited exposures to theological disciplines that would have taught all of us better. We are not too proud or arrogant to humbly admit we were wrong; for like all generations of men—past, present, and future—we have to learn to think **God's** thoughts after Him and learn His ways. This means forsaking our **own** thoughts and ways for **His**!

Chapter 6

The Holy Spirit: He Who Runs and Endows the Church

Many traditionalists believe the Bible furnishes no instance of a woman preaching or praying in a "mixed group" and perhaps there may be others who share this opinion, even though there are **many** such instances recorded in the Scriptures. But so as not to **further** confuse them by relating **all** of them, let us simply limit ourselves to just **one**. Probably the most **important instance** of men and women praying and preaching **together** was in the Upper Room fellowship prior to Pentecost as recorded in Acts 1:12-14, and on the Day of Pentecost as recorded in Acts 2:1-18.

In view of this **one instance**, how anyone can maintain that women are **not** called to preach and pray as members of the Body of Christ escapes many of **us** completely! Despite **any** arguments to the contrary by pragmatists as to what may be considered the successful ministries of many women or the **lack** of what may be considered a successful ministry is **not really** the determining factor of this discussion; for human beings cannot accurately adjudicate the success of **anyone's** ministry! Indeed, we see just the **outward** appearance, and that only "through a glass darkly"; so with our many human limitations, we are in **no** position to make such a judgment. We **are**, however, able to proclaim again the blessed assurance of a clear and unmistakable biblical response from the Lord Himself in Acts 2:17-18:

> And it shall come to pass in the last days, **saith God**, I will pour out of my spirit upon **all** flesh: and your sons **and your daughters shall prophesy**, and your young men shall see visions, and your old men shall dream dreams: and on my servants **and on my handmaidens** I will pour out in those days of my spirit, **and they shall prophesy**.

As to Gamaliel's advice to the Council concerning its counsel to put the Apostles to death, such advice showed the wisdom and insight of this distinguished scholar of the Law. It was **not God's** advice, it was **Gamaliel's**; but it was **good advice**, and if it had not been so recognized by the Council perhaps many of the Apostles would have been killed. Gamaliel was **not wrong**; for unlike the followers of the false leaders Theudas and Judas, the Apostles were witnessing to the Messiah, the Anointed of God, Jesus of Nazareth as Prince and Saviour, and the Holy Spirit gave such witness to their ministry that it cut the Council members to their hearts! Today, the Holy

Spirit gives witness to the ministry of some women who preach Christ, the Anointed of God; it actually cuts some people to **their** hearts, and they take counsel to discredit or ignore their message and calling! They do not seek to silence these women by killing them as did the Council to the Apostles; no, today they seek to silence them by barring them from the pulpits of the Lord's Church and inflicting upon them such intimidations and fellowship reprisals that many actually are afraid to even acknowledge the gifts of prophecy and exhortation bestowed upon them by the Holy Spirit!

Well might those who oppose women exercising such gifts consider the counsel of Gamaliel: "And now I say unto you, refrain from these (women), and let them alone: for if this counsel or this work be of me; it will come to nought: but if it be of God, ye cannot overthrow it; lest haply ye be found even to fight against God" (Acts 5:38-39).

In a world dominated by evil and controlled by the evil one, a lot of wicked things prosper, and **this** accounts for the rapid growth of the Jehovah's Witnesses and all other spurious sects. However, just as we can count on the evil one to give "success" to those who stand **against** the Gospel of Jesus Christ, praise the Lord, we can count on the Holy Spirit to give "success" to those who stand up **for** the Gospel of Christ, and that success is measured by **Him** in the accomplishment of **His** will!

Of course, it is true that the impulse of the Spirit in our lives must **always** be regulated by the rule of the Spirit given in God's Word; for the Holy Spirit does not lead anyone to do anything that He forbids in His Word, and **nowhere** in the Scriptures can you find the Holy Spirit forbidding women from sharing any of the spiritual gifts He imparts to believers simply because they are females and not males. Indeed, we have well established in previous responses that the Holy Spirit operates the Church **above all human prejudices and physical differences** between its members, and this is certainly one of the cardinal truths revealed to us concerning Him in the inerrant Word of God!

There is **no** question by the members of the Body of Christ that the Bible was written by men divinely inspired by God; but our problem arises from the **inability** of some of the members to **rightly divide** the Word of truth so that we can **all** understand God's will and way as over against man's will and man's way! The two are definitely **different** and it becomes our responsibility to forsake **ours** for **His**!

We have all been challenged by the Holy Spirit to leave the "calling" of ministers completely and exclusively in **His** hands! Indeed, this is where **Christ left** this responsibility; this is where the Scriptures say it **always has been** in spite of our **convictions and traditions** in proclaiming that **we** had a right to **withhold** that "calling" from women! Where did we go wrong? How is it possible that we could have been **so wrong for so long**? We have always accepted as Gospel truth the denial of the gifts of prophecy and exhortation to women in the Body of Christ, and we are embarrassed and distressed by the revelation of an **ancient truth** so **fundamental** to our faith, that it reveals one of our cherished traditions as being **heretical and unscriptural**! Again, the question is pertinent: Where did we go wrong?

To begin the answer, you can trace the problem back to the concept or belief that Christ left the church in the hands of the Apostles, and they were to control its operations until He returns for Her at the Rapture. This is **not true**, and John 14:16-18 makes it clear that the Holy Spirit took the **place** of Jesus as Leader in the lives of His believers and that they were to be subject to the instructions of the Holy Spirit who would "teach them all things, and bring all things to their remembrance" whatsoever **Jesus** said to them (John 14:26). Just before His ascension back to heaven, Jesus instructed His disciples in Acts 1:4-8 not to depart from Jerusalem but to wait there for their New Leader to take charge of them. That **New Leader** was the **Holy Spirit** and **not any** of the Apostles!

It stands to reason that Christ would **never** leave His precious, **infinite** Spiritual Body in the control of **finite** men; for **they** would be **no match** for the principalities, powers, rulers of the darkness of this world or spiritual wickedness in high places, **no match whatsoever**! Indeed, they needed Someone to even **remind** them of what they had **already learned** from Jesus. They were in **desperate** need of day-to-day instruction, moment-by-moment guidance, and hour-by-hour protection, and only the Holy Spirit could do this for them. To even **think** that Christ would turn the administrative operations of His Church from His hands into the hands of mere humans is **inconceivable**! The Church must do battle with a spiritual enemy **so powerful** that the human intelligence can't even **begin** to **comprehend** that kind of power, let alone **contend** with it. Members of the Church are beings who even after becoming children of God through spiritual rebirth, still don't even know how to **pray as they ought** to their Heavenly Father, except for the guidance and direction of the Holy Spirit. Indeed, if they don't have the spiritual capacity on their own to do something as simple as just **praying**, surely you cannot expect them to have the capacity to direct the vast administrative operations of the Church of Christ that moves on spiritual dimensions of infinity and eternity!

Thank the Lord, God is still in charge in the Person of the Holy Spirit, and He alone determines who shall preach the Gospel for the salvation of sinners and the edification of saints! Once you come to realize **Who is** in charge, **Who is** running the operations, **Who is** in control of the Church, and that because He is God, as the Third Person of the Trinity, **then** you come to **understand** that men make **no policy** decisions, give **no** counsel or advice, but have **absolutely nothing** to say in the administrative operations of the Church—for their job is to do what they are **told**: to carry out or implement orders, and serve where they are commanded. **Who** will preach, **when** they preach, **where** they preach, or even **how** they preach **is none of our business**; for these are **exclusively** the determinations of the Holy Spirit, and His **alone** to make! Not Peter, not James, not John, not Paul, not Matthew, not Luke, nor **any** of the other Apostles, prophets, evangelists, pastors, and teachers that the Holy Spirit gives for the edifying of the Church, **none of them**, I repeat **none of them**, have the authority to determine **who shall preach**.

When the Scriptures ask: "How shall they preach except they be **sent**?" (Romans 10:15a), the "sent" are those who receive the gifts of prophecy and exhortation from the Holy Spirit. He **alone** gives the gifts, and He **alone "sends"** the recipient of those gifts out to **preach**! No matter what you **heard** to the contrary, no matter what you **thought you read** in the Scriptures, no matter what **tradition** has dictated in the past, and no matter what your **personal convictions** are in this matter, no human being determines **who shall preach** the Gospel of Jesus Christ—**only** the **Holy Spirit**!

To even **think** otherwise, it will ultimately lead you to the theological position of the Roman Catholic Church, which believes that the Apostle Peter was given charge and control of the Church by Jesus when He ascended; and that Peter's successors, as Vicars of Christ (the Popes), have the divine authority to determine **who** shall preach as priests of God. This theological position makes the pope's edicts, encyclicals, pontifications and determinations **equal** with the Holy Scripture, and must be justified by the belief of the **infallibility** of the pope. To be sure, as Protestants we have not **yet** gone **this** far in our theology, and perhaps we would not; but that would **have** to be the **ultimate** resolution and conclusion of a belief that **man** is in control of the Church and thus determines who will be Her preachers and priests.

Persons who stand in the way of those who have been called to preach just because they are women shall surely have to give an account to the Lord for quenching the Holy Spirit by hindering His messengers and preventing the Gospel from going forth for the salvation of lost souls. It is a gravely serious and sobering matter to contemplate; that **many** Christians shall be **severely reprimanded** by Christ for preventing the laborers **He** has sent into **His** vineyard of service from doing the work **He** assigned them! Jesus told us to pray to the Lord of the harvest to send forth laborers into His harvest, and many members of the Body of Christ are faithfully doing this, and when the Lord **answers** their prayers and **sends** forth laborers, some **prevent** them from serving and working simply because they are **women**! Be assured; they will answer to the Lord for this interference and hindrance to the Kingdom's work in this world, and many lost souls will be required at their hands!

There are those who say, "If the Lord wants me to recognize a woman as a minister, He will have to personally show me!" Many who say this are very sincere, but they are also **sincerely wrong**! The Holy Spirit is **not** obligated in **any** way to show **you personally** above and beyond what He has **already clearly revealed** of Himself in His Word concerning His will and way in the administration of the Church. Who do **you** think you **are**? Why do you think you have **any** authority to question **His right** to dispense spiritual gifts of prophecy and exhortation to **women** as well as **men**! Must we continue to exhibit our lack of faith in the sovereignty of the Holy Spirit, as did the religious leaders to the sovereignty of Jesus when they said, "We would see a sign from thee. But Jesus answered and said unto them, 'an evil and adulterous generation seeketh after a sign: and there shall no sign be given to it, but the sign of the prophet Jonas'" (Matthew 12:39). A greater than Jonas is here; a greater than Solomon is here; a greater than Peter is here; and a greater than Paul is here; that Greater One now is the Holy Spirit, resident in the Church and controlling, in His sovereign power, Her **complete** operations in the world. What **more** do we seek to know;

indeed, what **more** can be said; what greater **assurance** do we need?

To those who say, "Well, I just **prefer** men preachers to women preachers; men as ministers to women as ministers; men as pastors to women as pastors; that's **my preference**, and that's the way I **see** it!" Respectfully, we would inquire of such persons: Who **asked** you? Who **cares** about **your preference or** the way **you see** it? Surely, the Holy Spirit does **not**, and **He's** the One who makes such decisions! You may find **ample** support and consensus for your position among other **members** of the Church, but their opinions and preferences do **not** matter any **more** than does **yours**! The Church is not a **democracy** controlled by the opinions and preferences of the members; no, the Church is a **theocracy** controlled **alone** by the Holy Spirit, and He not only doesn't **care** about our preferences or opinions but looks upon them with disdain, because if they are not **His** then they are all **wrong** and are not worthy of even being **thought** of, and certainly not to be ever verbalized and executed.

With the coming of the Holy Spirit at Pentecost, there also came into being a new **empowerment** to the Church that began a Revolution that Its enemies said was "turning the world upside down"; actually, we know that this Revolution was turning the world **right-side-up**! A significant part of that Revolution was the raising of the status of womanhood to the level of spiritual equality with manhood. This was a **new** concept to the **ancient** world, but it is an **old** concept to the **modern** world, and this "ancient revolution in the modern pulpit" can make a fantastic contribution to the Kingdom of God in the garnering of precious souls in such numbers we **never**

dreamed possible! The means to accomplish this fantastic feat, of eternal ramifications, is the **availability** of many more workers in the vineyard of service of prophecy and exhortation to the Holy Spirit for His use in a world of five billion souls, and where more than four billion of that five billion are living and dying without the knowledge of Christ as their personal Saviour.

Tremendous inroads can be made into the ranks of the unsaved if individual Christians will let the Holy Spirit take complete control of their lives, and if collective Christians will let the Holy Spirit take complete control of their local congregation.

The importance of this Revolution demands that we repeat:

> The Church would be utterly shocked to learn how many women, through the years, have been given the gifts of prophecy and exhortation but were afraid to acknowledge their calling because of strong opposition from their church, their pastor, their husband, their children, their families, other Christian women, and from the society of unbelievers. The tragedy represented by this great loss to the Kingdom of God can best be measured in the many souls who have already gone into a Christless eternity and the countless numbers for which that same eternal destiny is just a matter of time! However, it also shows itself in the many frustrated women who cause their families untold sufferings because they secretly carry the burden of these spiritual gifts without ever exercising or using them; so they never have peace of mind or the contentment of heart that comes from the assurance of

living in the center of God's will. The tremendous Revolution that would occur in our churches today to bring about a spiritual renaissance that would surpass our highest hopes to reach the lost before our Lord's return can still possibly come to pass if **we** can just get out of the way and let the Holy Spirit use **all** of the available resources without our prejudicial restraints that would hinder!

In a recent survey wherein the most important persons in history who have influenced the people of the world were rated, the Apostle Paul was rated **above Jesus** as the most influential contributor to the Christian faith. This is always what will happen when people think that men are in charge of the Church rather than the Holy Spirit! Because Paul wrote most of the New Testament Books, the survey concluded that he was the greatest leader of Christianity, not understanding that **all** New Testament Scriptures were inspired by the Holy Spirit who speaks for Christ!

The fact that this controversy **ever** arose is because men are "running the Church," and just as soon as we are willing to turn the control of It over to the Holy Spirit, this controversy will cease!

Chapter 7

Satanic Oppositions and Spiritual Realities

The Scripture proclaims, "For after that in the wisdom of God, the world by wisdom knew not God, it pleased God by the foolishness of **preaching** to save them that believe" (1 Corinthians 1:21).

Unfortunately, by design of tradition, many have deliberately cut off and therefore greatly limited our supply of preachers. Preaching or prophecy is one of the nineteen spiritual gifts given to the Church by the Holy Spirit, and He gives them to the Members of the Church without regard to the race, gender, age, education, or economic status of the recipient. It is **exclusively** His prerogative to dispense them as He sees fit, and He does it precisely "For the perfecting of the saints, for the work of the ministry, for the edifying of the Body of Christ" (Ephesians 4:12).

I formerly believed that this terrible tradition was so strongly upheld by many because of a lack of theological discipline; indeed, no one who has had exposure to the most basic and elementary study of biblical theology would **ever** put such limitations on the Godhead; they simply **know** better, and one would have to admit that those who insist on upholding this limitation are those who, for whatever reason, have been denied the blessing of study in biblical theology.

I am, however, now convinced that this is only a part of the reason; for the genesis of the problem is a lot **deeper** than that. Indeed, there are many pastors and ministers and countless lay people who have not had **any** theological training whatsoever, but they **clearly** understand the sovereignty of God to give spiritual gifts to whomever He wills!

I honestly believe that the problem is basically satanic in its origin; a hellish tradition straight out of perdition that has blinded the eyes of many to the tremendous limitations it imposes on the Church of Christ to carry out the command imperatives of the Great Commission of our Lord in Matthew 28:19, 20. Satan knows that the ranks of the preachers would more than **triple** if the restrictions of this tradition were lifted!

Jesus said, "The harvest truly is great, but the laborers are few; pray ye therefore the Lord of the harvest, that he would send forth laborers into his harvest" (Luke 10:2). But when God answers our prayers for more laborers and sends them to us, we categorically **reject** them because they don't meet **our** standards of race, gender, age, education, or economic status, and particularly gender; indeed, when God answers our prayers, we tell **Him** we reject **His** answer to our need for more laborers because they are women and we don't believe in women ministers! Imagine **us** telling **God!**

Jesus also said, "For what shall it profit a man, if he shall gain the whole world, and lose his own soul? Or what shall a man give in exchange for his soul?" (Mark 8:36, 37) It becomes increasingly obvious that those who perpetuate this horrible tradition fail to understand that Jesus is saying if you should gain possession and ownership of the whole world (cosmos), that is, **all** the physical creation (billions of galaxies—heavenly real estate that is so vast it has to be measured in terms of light years), it is not worth the value of **one** single solitary human soul! Now, if the price tag on a soul is **that** great, surely no Christian should be guilty of hindering the spread of the Gospel that **alone** can save that soul or **any other soul!**

This diabolical tradition also manifests itself in the lack of understanding of many to the very **nature** of the Church, the Body of Christ. Again, we see the problem basically as satanic in origin rather than educational because Nicodemus, a ruler of the Jews and a well-educated man, did **not** understand the message or mission of Jesus to be implemented through individuals who make up the Church as **spiritual entities**. When Jesus explained that such individuals had to be "born again," He had to explain to Nicodemus "that which is born of the flesh is flesh, and that which is born of the spirit is spirit" (John 3:6).

There is a distinct difference and dichotomy between the two, and those who fail to see this distinction by citing the **physical/social** (that which is born of flesh) as a basis for participation or non-participation in the varied ministries of the Church, fail to comprehend the basic **spiritual** nature of the Body of Christ and therefore play right into Satan's hands!

If you look at the Church as a **physical/social** entity, you will never truly appropriate its many spiritual blessings, powers, and promises for the accomplishment of its mission, and you will never understand or be able to contend with its enemies, which are **not** flesh and blood (physical), but **spiritual!** "For we wrestle not against flesh and blood: but against principalities, against powers, against the rulers of the darkness of this world, against spiritual wickedness in high places" (Ephesians 6:12). A lack of understanding of these basic facts concerning the nature of our enemies leaves us vulnerable to their attacks and puts us at a distinct disadvantage in contending with them.

It is **extremely** unfortunate that some of the words of the Apostle Paul are used as a rationale for preventing God's choices—those He has ordained—from exercising their prophetic gift. Indeed, I'm sure the Great Apostle must cringe in his spirit at our lack of understanding of his personal process of spiritual development in the Arabian desert which enabled him to see from God's perspective and vantage point rather than from that of men or culture (cf. Galatians 1:11—2:11ff.; 2 Corinthians 12:1-5ff.). God's ways and thoughts are simply **not** like ours, and all of the great patriarchs, prophets, apostles, and disciples who were used by God to manifest His will and way to the world had to learn this **basic spiritual lesson**, and the Apostle Paul was **no exception!**

In all the writings of Scripture, the Holy Spirit never hides the facts of **any** of His servants' spiritual growth and development to the point where they start thinking God's thoughts after Him, and not their own thoughts, opinions, and ideas. After all, what Jesus brought to the world in the founding of the Church and almost everything connected with it was entirely different from anything this world had experienced before. This is what He meant when He talked about the old wine-skins not being able to contain the new wine; or the inability of the old cloth to facilitate the new patch. His Gospel and His Church so significantly broke down the many existing barriers that separated mankind that it was said of the Apostolic Church, "these that have turned the world upside down are come hither also" (Acts 17:6b).

Any serious student of the Bible can understand and appreciate the Apostle Paul's abrupt and progressive development from his views of Judaism denying the right of women to even speak or say **anything** in public religious assembly (that restriction **was** in conformity with men's traditions) to the point where as a follower of Christ he later advises women who prophesy and pray **in the Church assembly** to cover their heads. Now this is the **same Apostle Paul** who according to his Jewish teachings and practices had previously forbidden women a place of equality. But now he can see the issue from the perspective of Christ Jesus.

Listen to him declare, "There is neither Jew nor Greek, there is neither bond nor free, there is neither **male** nor **female**: for ye are all one in Christ Jesus" (Galatians 3:28). Paul is now sure-footed about the way God looks at His people! Finally, in the closing days of his ministry, hear Paul exhorting the brethren: "Help those women (Euodias and Syntyche) which laboured with me **in the Gospel**" (Philippians 4:3a). The Apostle Paul had to learn that God is no respecter of persons, and **we** have to learn that God is no respecter of persons, just as Paul did; and it is a sign of spiritual immaturity when we have **not** learned that lesson!

> For my thoughts are not your thoughts, neither are your ways my ways, saith the Lord. For as the heavens are higher than the earth, so are my ways higher than your ways, and my thoughts higher than your thoughts (Isaiah 55:8, 9).

God simply does not think as we think, and it is **He** who says:

> It shall come to pass after this that I will pour out my spirit upon **all** flesh; your sons **and** your **daughters** shall prophesy; your old men shall dream dreams, and your young men shall see visions, even upon the servants **and maids** I will, in those days, pour out my spirit (Joel 2:28, 29).

And on the very day God officially gave to the Church His Holy Spirit, He reiterated the fulfillment of this promise first spoken through the mouth of His Prophet Joel; now through the mouth of His Apostle Peter:

> And it shall come to pass in the last days, saith God, I will pour out of my spirit upon all flesh: and your sons and your daughters shall prophesy, and your

young men shall see visions, and your old men shall dream dreams: and on my servants and on my handmaidens I will pour out in those days of my spirit; and they shall prophesy (Acts 2:17, 18).

We **all** know what Paul said, and some of us understand why he said what he said; but in the Joel 2 and Acts 2 passages, **God Himself** is speaking! It is **God** who says, "they shall prophesy"; why then should **any** of us say, "They shall **not** prophesy!" God says, "they shall," and we say, "they shall **not**!" There is no question in our minds as to Who is right, Who is telling the truth, and who is lying!

It is interesting to notice and observe that those who are most vocal, intransigently standing in greatest opposition to women exercising the gift of prophecy in the Church, and who would deny them access to the pulpits of our many traditionalist churches, simply because they are women, would **themselves be so denied** if they were members of most of the other major Protestant denominations; not because of their gender, but because of their race or education or, more precisely, because of their **lack** of it! Indeed, **all** the other major denominations require that those who exercise the gift of prophecy in their pulpits **must** have four years of college and three years of professional seminary training before they even can be ordained to serve with official standing as a minister of the Church, and this rule is even **more** stringently applied as it relates to the position of pastor in the churches of other denominations.

If such a rule were enacted in the traditionalist churches, then 90% of our pastors and ministers would be denied access to the pulpits of the churches holding this tradition. Yet these **same men** have the audacity to deny those whom **God Himself** has "called" and uses to win, by their prophetic calling, precious souls to the Kingdom of God!

It is incredible and unbelievable to contemplate the **magnitude** of the **consequences** this traditional antithesis brings to what the **very** mouth of the Lord has spoken; even though we are accused of making too much of the tradition and taking it too seriously, what is more important in this life than the salvation of precious souls? That is why any traditions of men that hinder souls from hearing the Gospel must be looked upon with deadly seriousness.

To be sure, it is equally wrong for these many other denominations to deny those whom the Lord has called and ordained the right to exercise their spiritual gift of prophesy or preaching simply because they lack formal educational credentials; for they shut out all the Amoses whom God Himself has raised up among them to proclaim His Word; but at least they have studied the Scriptures enough to understand that God has **the last Word in all things!** If He says He will pour out of His Spirit on **all flesh**, and that both **sons and daughters**—both **men and women**—shall prophesy then that is the way it is; indeed, that is the way **it must be!**

The Church was founded and formulated in the mind and will of God; She is **His** thing, and He does **not** need **any** man to tell Him how to operate Her, or who He should call to perpetuate Her message! It is bad to not know, and even worse not to realize that you don't know; but thanks be to God, we can **all** be sure and **know**; **whatever God says, it is right, and it is true!** When our Lord spoke to the Seven Churches that are representative of every Church Age, as recorded in Revelation 2 and 3, the last words He said to all seven of them were "He that hath an ear, let him hear what the Spirit says to the churches."